How to Avoid Making Bad Business Decisions

Entrepreneur Book Series

Colvin Nyakundi

Mendon Cottage Books

Disclaimer

The information in this book is provided for informational purposes only and it is not intended for use as a substitute for proper financial or legal direction by a qualified financial or legal advisor. The information is believed to be accurate as presented based on research by the author.

No claims of income are given and examples are used to portray the ideas of the author as possibilities without representing actual earnings that can be made.

The author or publisher is not responsible for financial loss or damage incurred by implementing ideas mentioned in this book. The author or publisher is not responsible for errors or omissions that may exist.

Warning

The Book is for informational purposes only and before starting or running any business, it is recommended that you consult with your financial or legal professional. Always follow all laws and regulations regarding taxes, selling, buying, or ecommerce.

Table of Contents

Introduction...4

Predicting the Outcome of a Business Decision.............................6

Venturing Into a New Business Environment................................8

How to Secure Your Business..12

Legal and Ethical Issues...16

Who Can Help You Make the Right Decision................................19

Steps Involved In Making Decisions...22

Conclusion...24

Author Bio...25

Publisher...36

How to Avoid Making Bad Business Decisions

Introduction

If you're an investor or have been involved in any type of business, then you probably know that all entrepreneurs make several decisions each day. Some of the decisions that entrepreneurs make include the quantity and brand of products to buy, the selling price of the products and the kind of business to invest in. whether you're the owner of the business or just an employee, you may be required to decide the number and qualifications of assistants to hire. You might also be required to decide which employees to layoff if the business isn't performing very well.

In some instances, several competing entities might decide to merge so as to stay ahead of all the other competitors. This means that as the owner or the one in charge of the business, you might be forced to decide who to partner with and who to avoid. With this and many more decisions that entrepreneurs make, you must learn how to avoid making bad business decisions.

With good business decisions, you can be sure that your company is not at any risk of collapsing. The decision you make can also help you avoid lawsuits or conmen who might be looking for an opportunity to swindle you. However, if you make bad business decisions, you risk losing some or all your employees or even your customers. Illegal business decisions might also land you in jail or even force you to shut down the business. You must therefore be very careful and take your time before making any decision.

The book 'How to Avoid Making Bad Business Decisions' is designed to help entrepreneurs make the best decisions in their day to day activities. Regardless of whether you're an established businessman or an aspiring investor, you need to read this book so that you can know where you're going wrong when making decisions. By simply reading this book, you can significantly increase your profits and even expand your business to new territories.

The book will guide you on how to make a business decision in a new environment, how to predict the outcome of a decision you're about to make and who to consult before making any serious decision.

Enjoy reading the book 'How to Avoid Making Bad Business Decisions!!!'

Predicting the Outcome of a Business Decision

Apart from helping you strategize on how to run a business in future, accurate prediction will help you know when something is about to go wrong in the company or business. This means that you should invest some of your resources, time and energy towards making sure that you have accurate prediction of the outcome of a decision you're about to make.

The first thing you need to do is analyze the risk you'll be taking by making a given decision. In most cases, the higher the risk involved, the more the returns you're likely to get. However, with increased risk, you might lose some or even all of the money that you've invested. Therefore, by knowing the risk involved, you can easily know what the future holds for your business. If you aren't experienced in risk analysis, it is advisable that you seek the services of professionals such as actuaries.

You can also predict the outcome of a business decision by simply analyzing past experiences. This could be other people's experiences or even your own experiences. If somebody else achieved something after making a given decision, you're also likely to achieve the same thing if you make a similar decision. If somebody hired five workers but they couldn't manage to handle a given task, what makes you think that the task will be accomplished if you're the one hiring five employees?

It is also possible to predict the future after looking at how experts react after large companies and businesses have made certain decisions. For example, if two competing companies decide to merge, analysts normally converge and try to discuss how the new entity is likely to fair after the merger. Analysts discuss such issues in forums such as TV shows, internet and newspaper articles, and during seminars. By simply watching what these analysts have to say, you can easily know the outcome of a given business decision.

Entrepreneurs can also predict the outcome of a given business decision by being observant of their immediate environment and current happenings. For example, the rate at which businesses grow might depend on several factors including the current political situation, security in the area and government policy. Therefore, by simply observing your immediate environment you can be able to know whether your business is going to perform well or not.

Hurriedly made decisions are not always the best. You can therefore predict the outcome of your business decision by considering how long it took you to make the decision. To be sure that you're making the right decision, it is always advisable that you take as much time as possible before making any commitments. You should also consult as widely as possible when required to make a decision.

Venturing Into a New Business Environment

It is every entrepreneur's wish to expand their territory and offer their products and services to as many people as possible. However, expanding a business to new areas is not as easy as many people tend to think. You can't wake up one day and decide to open a branch of your business in a new area. To begin with you probably don't know your competitors in the new area. You also don't know the preferences of the people in the new territory. With this and many more challenges, investors must be very careful or else risk making losses.

When venturing into a new area, you need to decide when exactly you're going to start selling your products and/or services. You also need to know the approximate number of employees required to help you run the business. You must also decide the type of products to start selling or the nature of services to offer. Before the business is officially launched in the new area, you must decide who to partner with and how you're going to relate with the local authorities. With all these and many more decisions to be made, you certainly have to be very cautious when expanding your business to new territories.

Before setting up any business, it is always advisable that you abide by all the laid down government rules and procedures. Remember that each political area has different laws and regulations. You must therefore never assume that the laws that were applicable in your original markets will also be applicable in the new territory. If possible, you should consult a lawyer who's conversant with the laws applicable in the new area. The lawyer will help you know what you're expected to do and what you're expected not to do once the business is operational.

The next thing you need to do is make sure that you have data about the approximate number of people in need of the products or services you're offering. You should also know the number of companies or business offering the same products and services. With this crucial data, you can be able to strategize on how to penetrate the new environment. With the approximate number of potential clients, you can be able to avoid overstocking or under-stocking your products. On the other hand, if you know the number of competitors, you can easily know the number of marketing agents to hire.

You must also analyze consumers' purchasing power before venturing into a new territory. A consumer's purchasing power is the amount of cash that an average consumer is able and willing to set aside for the acquisition of a given product or service. People in different geographical and/or political regions have different priorities and preferences in life. For example, some people might be more willing to spend their cash on television sets while other people prefer personal computers. If you know their preferences, you can easily know what to sell to them-no need to start selling products that nobody will buy. By analyzing the consumer's purchasing power in that area, you'll be able to know whether you'll make profit or losses.

Never underestimate your competitors when thinking of venturing into a new territory. Even if your brand is the most widely preferred in your current territory, you should not assume that you'll also dominate the new area. The only way you can successfully penetrate a new environment is by looking at what your competitors are doing and coming up with new marketing ideas. Strategic marketing involves observing your competitors shortcomings and upside and then coming up with unique ways of convincing potential clients to try your services or products. In other words, you need to take advantage of your competitor's weaknesses to portray your product as the best one. Be careful to avoid slandering the competitor(s) as they might decide to sue you for damages caused by your adverts.

You must have a contingency plan on how to survive until the business picks up. This basically means that you must never assume that you'll start making profits immediately. Don't be surprised to hear that even some of the most distinguished brands don't make profits from all their branches. As a matter of fact, some branches make consistent losses and the company decides to pull out of the new market within a few months of entry. Whenever thinking of opening a new branch, you must ensure that you have other sources of income to supplement you until the new branch starts making profits. Initially, you might be even forced to inject extra funds to pay workers.

Company CEOs are driven by the desire to dominate their territories and sell their products and services to as many people as possible. This means that they can do anything to make sure that you are out of the market. As a matter of fact, some companies implore unethical/illegal means just to make sure that their competitors are out of the market. Therefore, the only way you can penetrate a new market is by strategizing on how to counter propaganda against your products and or services. You must also put in place mechanisms to identify instances where your business is being sabotaged. If you aren't careful, you'll find it quite hard to venture into the new territory and start making profits.

It is also important to note that some consumers are apprehensive of new products and services. This is normally the case where a given company has garnered customer loyalty and hence most consumers are willing to purchase their products only. The only way you can penetrate such a market is by coming up with tactics to reassure potential customers that your products are the best and can't cause them any harm. You must also be willing to offer free sample products so that potential clients can know exactly what to expect. One of the worse decisions that investors make is assuming that anybody can buy any brand without thinking twice.

If you're thinking of venturing into a new area, you should never try to change consumer's principles and virtues. Rather than doing that, try to adjust your products to fit the new market. For example, in Islamic states women are expected to be fully covered up to the toes and wear a hijab. If you're selling a product targeting women, nobody will buy it if the packing has a picture of a woman wearing pants and with no headscarf. The only way you can attract more customers is by ensuring that the packaging respects their virtues and principles.

How to Secure Your Business

A secure business environment is one in which there is minimal probability of an accident, theft or anything that could cause damage to property or the brand. If you're keen on becoming a successful entrepreneur, you must never start a business and fail to secure it. With security, you can rest assured that everything will go as planned and that you'll be making consistent profits.

Regardless of the type of business, you should never do anything without a plan. A business plan is a set of ideas on how you plan to run the business, what you need in order to run the business and what you intend to achieve during a given period of time. After formulating a business plan, you must ensure that it is fully implemented and appropriate adjustments made if something didn't go as planned. A businessman with no plan is at a very high risk of making loses especially if something out of the norm happens.

In order to run a secure business, you must never ignore the importance of keeping records. Business records help trace all the transactions during a given period of time and hence it will be easier to trace where you lost some money. Records can also help you plan for the future as you'll know the products that are selling faster than others. By keeping accurate records, you can be able to observe customer preferences and hence know how you can enhance your sales through incentives.

Engaging in illegal businesses is one of the things you should never do. Even if it looks quite lucrative you should never even think of doing such businesses. This means that you must also avoid signing deals with criminals. Engaging in illegal businesses or signing deals with criminals exposes you to lawsuits and bad publicity. Your operating license can also be suspended or even canceled if you're ever caught doing illegal businesses.

When your business relies heavily on the internet, you must never assume that nobody can hack into your system. Even the most secured networks are always at risk of being hacked or compromised by saboteurs. Always ensure that you've installed and activateda strong antivirus and firewall. You can also hire a professional IT company to help you protect all devices. Apart from securing your devices and network, you need to educate your employees on how they should handle their personal information. Remember that anybody can access your employees' accounts if they have their username and password. You therefore ought to train them on how they can secure their passwords and make sure that nobody else knows the passwords.

The safety measures installed in your business premises also determine how secure the business is. You should always ensure that there is minimal risk of injury or destruction to property. The cost of treating injured workers is quite high especially if they're not insured. You therefore risk making loses if you have to take care of their medical bills after they've been injured while at work.

You must also invest in heavy security measures if you're determined to operate a secure business. With the ever increasing rate of violent robberies, you must ensure that your business is protected by all possible means. The stakes are much higher if you handle bulk cash transactions. One of the security measures you can put in place is to higher armored vehicles to transfer cash to the bank. No need to accumulate huge sums of money and then let somebody steal the cash. You can also hire armed security personnel to help protect the business from violent robberies.

Hiring trustworthy employees is also one of the ways in which you can make sure that your business is secure. You must never make the mistake of hiring employees randomly without ascertaining their history. You might end up hiring somebody who is a mole working for your competitors or somebody planning to steal from you.Before a new employee is allowed access to sensitive areas in the business, they must be fully vetted and be put under probation for several months. You can also hire private detectives to help do background checks before a new employee starts working.

Comprehensive insurance coverage is also one of the things that can help you run a secure business. With comprehensive insurance, you'll be compensated in case of accidents such as fires, injuries, theft or destruction of property by natural disasters. As a matter of fact, covering your business should be one of the top priorities before anything else.

Unsatisfied, underpaid and overworked employees won't ever be fully committed to work for a long period of time. In order to optimize your employees' performance, you must ensure that they work in a favorableenvironment. You're at risk of losing your employees' loyalty if you make them uncomfortable while at work. You'll therefore be running an insecure business as they can easily shift their loyalty and start working for your competitors.

Even if you're running a small business, you must never ignore the importance of patenting your ideas, branding your products and registering your trademark. Your creativity is something that should help you increase your profits. However, you can't lay claim to any idea that you haven't patented. This means that even your competitors can copy your ideas to increase their profits at your expense.

Legal and Ethical Issues

Business decisions are highly influenced by legal and ethical issues. Whereas legal issues are issues related to enacted laws, ethical issues are those dealing with acceptable standards of social or professional behavior.Ethical issues influence how the general population perceive your company and hence their willingness to purchase your products. On the other hand, legal issues determine whether you'll be sued by the government or disgruntled customers. This means that you can't decide to ignore the importance of making right legal decisions or ethically correct choices.

When making business decisions, you must always avoid legal battles at all costs. Apart from the fact that they're quite expensive, they portray your business negatively and hence you'll end up losing customers to your competitors. In case a federal or state court rules against you, you might be forced to suspend operations or even relocate the business elsewhere. If there is a disagreement between you and your competitors, employees or customers, you should try as much as possible to settle it out of court.

As an enthusiastic entrepreneur, you must never collude with your competitors to overprice products or services. Collusion is ethically and legally wrong. Once customers find out that you colluded to overcharge them, they will avoid your products and hence you can easily start making loses. You can also be sued by a customer for collusion to defraud the general public.

Bribery is also one of the things that you must never engage in for as long as you want to become a successful entrepreneur. On top of being illegal, the act of giving or receiving bribes is also ethically wrong. It is on record that managing directors of one of the largest companies in the US were forced to resign after details emerged about how they offered bribes on several occasions. Apart from being prosecuted, the incident portrayed the companies negatively and generally affected their sales. Even if your business fortunes are dwindling you must never consider giving or receiving bribes so as to gain favors from anybody.

So as to attract more customers, some manufacturers opt to lie about the ingredients contained in their products. However, this is one of the things that you must never do. On top of losing business due to bad publicity you might be charged in court for misrepresentation. Lying to customers could be beneficial in the short run but it is definitely disastrous in the long run.

Whether you've made the right or wrong decision you must always be a man of your own words. This means that you should stick to what you have said and what you've signed. You should never back down on a deal that you have signed with your competitors or anybody else. Doing so will portray you as a very untrustworthy businessman and hence nobody will be willing to do business with you in future. If the signed deal is legally binding, you might end up being sued for damages incurred after you declined to honor your part of the deal.

Each day, businessmen have to make several decisions on issues touching ethics and the law. You must therefore learn how to avoid people who can tempt you to do something unethical. When making decisions, the first thing that should be on your mind is customer satisfaction. Before implementing any decision, you must try to think of how the public is likely to react after details about your decisions emerge.

Different people in different parts of the world change their preferences and stand from time to time. Something that is deemed right currently could be viewed as wrong in the future. Therefore, you should never assume that you should always make the same decisions each day when it comes to ethics. The best thing to do is to be always updated on what most people prefer and what they hate.

Who Can Help You Make the Right Decision

Regardless of your level of experience on certain issues, it is never a bad idea to get advice from other people. Actually, it is always advisable that you seek advice from as many people as possible before making any decision. However, you need to be very careful when deciding who to seek advice from. The only way you can avoid making the wrong decisions is by seeking advice from people who have your best interests at heart. After getting advice, you shouldn't go ahead and implement it without challenging the validity of the advice you've received. All human beings are subject to error and hence you could have been misadvised. You therefore ought to be very careful on the decision you make after getting advice from other people. Keep in mind that you're solely responsible for all the decisions you make; your advisers won't be liable to the consequences of the decision you make.

When required to make a decision, you need to consult experts onthat field. If possible, you should get in touch with somebody who's made similar decisions in the past. After getting advice from somebody who's made a similar decision in the past, you have to analyze the impact of the decision that was made. If the decision resulted in something positive, you can go ahead and implement it. However, if the decision didn't achieve the intended goals, you should not try to implement it unless you know what went wrong.

All successful businessmen and women have mentors. A mentor is someone you trust to guide and advice you on critical matters in your day to day activities. Before making any decision, it is advisable that you get in touch with your mentor and get their opinion on the issue at hand. It is important that you be very careful when choosing your mentor. He/she should be somebody with high integrity standards and your best interests at heart.

You can also get business advice from your friends and family members. Advice from friends and family members is quite important in situations where the decision is likely to affect those close to you. For instance, you should consult your family before selling shares in a company or deciding to open a new branch. Your friends on the other hand can help you understand how the general public is likely to react to the decisions you make.

It is possible that you might be required to make decisions onmatters you have no jurisdiction over. In such case, you have to consult your superiors before signing any binding agreements. You can also consult your juniors if you have to make a decision on certain issues but you don't have particular details about the issue at hand. In this case, your juniors will help you understand the issue before youmaking any commitments. Juniors might be in a position to make better decisions than you because they're the ones directly involved in day to day running of the business or company. You should therefore never ignore their importance when it comes to decision making.

Your competitors can also help you make the right choice. However in this case you won't consult them; all that you'll do is observe their past decisions and how it affected their operations. After carefully analyzing their past decisions, you can easily know the kind of decisions that you ought not to make. In other words, you'll be learning from their mistakes and then put in place measures to avoid making similar mistakes.

Research firms can also help you make the right decision in several ways. To begin with, you can hire a research firm to carry out a survey about how people perceive certain issues or products. This way you'll know the kind of products that are widely preferred and hence invest more cash towards improving such products. You can also hire a research firm to investigate how your competitors managed to penetrate and maybe dominate the market. The firm will therefore come up with a list of ideas on what you should do in order to fully penetrate the market and increase your market share.

Right decisions can also be made based on information from news outlets, the internet and books. In this case, all you'll do is ensure that you watch news as frequently as possible and keep on adjusting your mode of operation to fit modern trends. You can also gather a lot of information about your business rivals and preferences of the average citizen from news outlets. You'll therefore be able to make an informed decision.

Steps Involved In Making Decisions

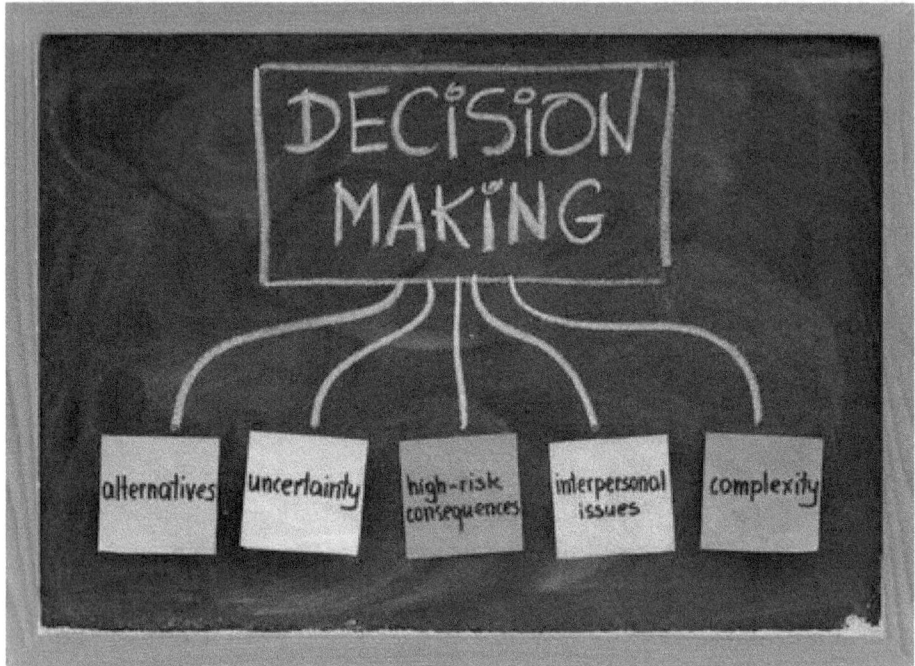

The first step in decision making involves identifying the problem at hand. This means that you need to know why you have to make the decision. What drove you to want to make that decision? For instance, if you're thinking of hiring extra personnel, you need to ask yourself the following questions: why do you need to hire extra personnel? What will happen if you don't hire them? By asking yourself the above questions, you'll know exactly why you need to make the decision and the consequences of not making the decision.

After identifying why you need to make the decision, you need to consider the time constraints in the decision you're about to make. When are you supposed to have made the decision? Can you postpone making the decision to a future date? The amount of time you have will influence the number of people you're likely to consult. If you have plenty of time to make the decision, you can consult as many people as you can. On the other hand, if you have limited time, then you need to talk to only those people who are conversant with the issue at hand.

The next step involves considering the options you have and the possible outcomes. This means that you'll be formulating ideas on how to solve the problem at hand. There could be several ways in which you can solve the problem. However, you should go for the option with high returns and minimal risks.

Do you have facts regarding the issue at hand? Before making any decision, you must always ensure that you have all the facts regarding the issue. If there is any ambiguity, you should seek clarification from concerned parties before making your final decision. If you ever try to make a decision without all the facts, you might end up making the wrong decision.

You're ready to make the decision if you've consulted all concerned parties, obtained relevant facts about the issue and sought advice from other people. Just consider the possible outcomes of each of the decisions you're about to make and then go ahead and make the best decision. After making the decision, you can go ahead and fully implement the resolutions made.

After implementing the resolutions, you need to obtain feedback about the impact of the decision on your business. Feedback will help you in case you need to make a similar decision infuture.

Conclusion

When doing business, it is very important that you avoid making decisions based on your emotions. Decisions should depend on available facts and not on emotions arising from your relationship with those affected by the decision. In other words, you should try as much as possible to avoid mixing business with your personal life. Your judgment could be clouded if you make decisions based on your emotions.

Even if the outcome wasn't what you expected, it doesn't mean that you made the wrong decision. It is possible that something could have changed after you made the decision. It is also possible that the outcome could be below par due to poor implementation of the resolutions made. You therefore have to go through the outcome and try to figure out what could have gone wrong.

Author Bio

Colvin Tonya Nyakundi

Colvin Tonya Nyakundi is a freelance writer and co-author of 'How to Avoid Making Bad Business Decisions' Apart from that book, he has a portfolio of several other publications accumulated in the more than two years that he has been freelancing through www.odesk.com.

He has authored several personal relationships, construction and real estate, lifestyle and travel and holiday guide publications. Other books that he has co-authored include 'How to Survive in the Woods', 'How to Start Making Money Online', 'How to Survive in a Desert', 'How to Improve Your Communication Skills,' 'Construction Guide for New Investors in Real Estate,' 'How to Make Your Backyard a Magnificent Venue for Hosting Events', 'How to Identify the Perfect Holiday Destination', "How Your Favorite Meal Could be Killing You Slowly" and 'How to Prepare and Survive in a Foreign Country.' You can get in touch with him through his official Facebook account, tonyanc@facebook.com.

Our books are available at

1. Amazon.com
2. Barnes and Noble
3. Itunes
4. Kobo
5. Smashwords
6. Google Play Books

Check out some of the other JD-Biz Publishing books

<u>Gardening Series on Amazon</u>

Health Learning Series

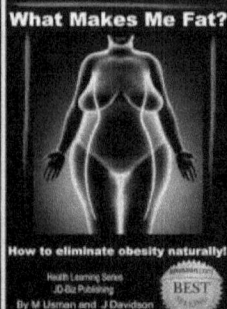

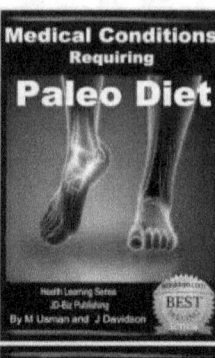

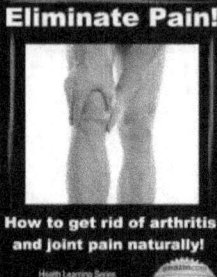

Learn To Draw Series

How to Build and Plan Books

Entrepreneur Book Series

Publisher

JD-BizCorp

P O Box 374

Mendon, Utah 84325

http://www.jd-biz.com/